The History of Britai:

BY

Stephan Weaver

Contents

The Return of the Christianity through St. Augustine —
597 A.D.

The Northumbrian Supremacy — A.D. 617

The Mercian Supremacy — A.D. 626-821

Viking Britain

First Invasion by the Vikings — A.D. 793

The Great Danish Army Invades Britain — 866- 877
A.D.

King Alfred Defeats the Vikings — A.D. 871

The Commencement of the Anglo-Saxon Chronicle —
890 A.D.

King Canute of Denmark Becomes King of England —
1016 A.D.

Medieval Britain

The Battle of Hastings — 1066

Magna Carta — 1215

The Hundred Years War with France — 1337-1453

The Black Death — 1348

The War of the Roses — 1455-1485

Tudor Britain

The Termination of the War of the Roses — 1485

Henry VIII Becomes King of England — 1509

The Formation of the Church of England — 1534

The Union of Wales and England — 1536

The Formation of the East India Company — 1600

Stuart Britain

James VI of Scotland and the I of England — 1603

1651 English Civil War — 1642

The Introduction of Tea in Britain —1652-1654

The Great Fire of London — 1666

The Great Revolution — 1688

Georgian Britain

Great Britain Appoints the First Prime Minister — 1721

The American Declaration of Independence — 1776

Act of Union — 1800

The Slave Trade Act — 1807

The Battle of Waterloo —1815

Victorian Britain

The Great Exhibition — 1851

The Crimean War — 1854

The Last Public Hanging — 1868

Education Act — 1870

Population of Britain 40 million — 1901

Modern Britain

World War I — 1914-1918

Ireland's Declaration of Independence — 1920

World War II — 1939-1945

Britain's partaking in the Gulf War — 1990

The Channel Tunnel — 1994

Introduction

History is boundless. Shaped by the various incidents that had transpired hundreds and thousands of years ago, our world is truly a fascinating entity. It is only natural for many of us to be engrossed in history and to remain eager to further our understanding of how and why our nations, neighboring and distant countries are the way they are today.

This book particularly focuses on the History of Britain. It contains a compilation of 50 significant events that occurred in Britain's history. It addresses the time from Prehistoric Britain to Modern Britain.

In the course of this book, you will find notable events that have befallen in Britain, such as the Roman invasion, the Vikings invasion, the Great Fire of London, the English Civil War and much more.

Prehistoric Britain

The era referred to as "prehistory" in Britain is prior to Britain joining the Roman Empire in A.D.43. This era existed for millennia.

Britain Becomes an Island — 6500 B.C.

Following the conclusion of the Ice Age, around 10,500 B.C., temperatures soared. Rising sea levels catalyzed by the melting ice separated Britain from the European mainland around 6500 B.C., and Britain became an island.

The dwellers in Britain then were Homo sapiens' descendants. Their arrival in the north part of Europe is estimated to be around 30,000-40,000 years ago. They made their living through gathering and hunting.

Neolithic (New Stone Age) — 4000-2400 B.C.

Neolithic or New Stone Age is most commonly used in connection with agriculture, which is the period when cereal cultivation and animal domestication was introduced in Britain. The inhabitants of that era made began to cultivate crops. It is usually thought that Britain's introduction to farming mainly emanated from massive immigration from the Channel. Studies of DNA, today, indicates that the exodus wasn't probably that much. From the entire population, the newcomers accounted for 20%.

So the preponderance of farmers was most likely the people of Mesolithic. They adapted new ways of living which they exported to Britain's mainland. Rather than a sudden change, archeological records demonstrate that the adaptation of agriculture resulted from gradual changes.

The dissemination of farming, throughout the British Isles, took about two millennia.

The Middle Neolithic (c. 3300-2900 B.C.)

The Middle Neolithic saw the establishment of splendid chamber tombs, the growth of cursus monuments, and the development of causewayed enclosure. There are also the first individual burials and stone circles.

The end of the Neolithic

Around the dusk of the Neolithic era, there was an introduction of Copper metallurgy, which signaled the transition period of the Bronze Age— sometimes called the Chalcolithic or Eneolithic Era. Bronze was widely employed at that time as the primary material for tools and weapons, making stone technology obsolete. This signaled the end of the era of Neolithic and thus the Stone Age.

The Bronze Age — 2400 B.C.

Britain, around 2400 B.C., saw fresh practices and beliefs which was called the Beaker 'Package'. This came in Britain through cross-channel relations with Europe, bringing with it new people, technology, burial rites, objects and most importantly the talent of working with gold metal and copper.

Copper was initially employed to produce items. Then, around 2200 B.C., bronze (which has greater hardness than copper, a lower melting point and better casting properties) was made by blending copper with tin. Gradually, bronze supplanted stone and became the primary material for producing tools. By 2200 B.C., Britain's Early Bronze Age had begun.

The deceased of the Early Bronze Age in Britain were buried under earth mounds (called barrows), frequently along with a beaker beside their body. Cremation was later on acclimatized— making it a new funeral practice. Evidence discovered from about 1100 B.C. explaining the funeral practices of the departed is scanty, yet the usage of cremation continued. The Bronze Age's inhabitants built several famous prehistoric sites including the Stonehenge in southern England as well as Seahenge.

Britain's early Bronze Age houses were round and contained a pointed top with a single entrance. The walls of these houses were made of woods and the roof was thatched with straws or reeds. These houses contained one room. Many houses of this era had a hearth at the center for light, cooking and heat purposes.

The Bronze Age populace consumed cattle, sheep, pigs, deer, shellfish and birds.

The Stonehenge — 2800 B.C.

Stonehenge is undoubtedly the most crucial and celebrated Neolithic monument in the whole of Britain and Europe dating from 2800 B.C. It remains as a timeless monument to people who constructed it. The Stonehenge that we see today was erected in 4 main steps from 2800 B.C. - 1550 B.C. This is deemed to have been an astronomical calendar or a shrine to the moon, sun, stars and planets.

Avebury and Stonehenge, two of the most popular circular monuments are situated in Wessex. Stonehenge was constructed over a time of 1700 years.

Stages of Stonehenge

First Phase:

Phase one commenced around 2800 B.C. and embraced a ditch and bank over ninety meters across. It has a succession of fifty-six punctures and an opening within the bank. Also, on the exterior of the entrance, the heel stone was built in the course of this stage.

Second Phase:

The second phase began around 2100 B.C. which included the four station stones situated in a rectangle. Some 82 bluestones from the Prescelly Mountains were transported to the site. The weight of the bluestones is up to 4 tons each.

Third Phase:

It was around 2000 B.C. that the third stage began, and it saw the arrival of the Sarsen stones, which were transported from the Marlborough Downs newar Avebury, in north Wiltshire, about 25 miles north of Stonehenge. The biggest of the Sarsen stones transported to Stonehenge weigh 50 tonnes.

The Final Phase:

After 1500 BC, the final phase soon took place when the bluestones were repositioned in the horseshoe and circle that we witness today. Originally, the bluestone circle was probably around 60— these have long since been fragmented or removed. Some remain merely as stumps below ground level.

The Celtic People Arrive in Britain — 500 B.C.

The Indo-Europeans who invaded Britain were Celtic tribes, kinsmen of the Gauls in France. Their invasion continued for many centuries.

The earlier tribes of them who settled in Britain and Ireland were Gaels, raiding or assimilating with the previous settlers.

Other Celtic tribes, the Britons, came to Britain about 400 B.C. They drove the Gaels into the lands of Scotland and Wales and settled in England themselves. The name Briton and Britain originates from these people.

England remained settled devoid of any raids for several centuries, bestowing the Britons a period of settlement and a chance to advance their civilization.

The lowlands of England were rife with forest and marshes. So the tribes lived scattered adjacent to valleys where drier land existed.

The Celts were a civilized class that knew how to cultivate land, mine, weave wool into cloth, work iron and create iron weapons. The families of chieftains wore brightly colored wardrobes and were embellished with marvelous metal ornaments such as bracelets and necklaces.

Although Britons were a united force, they were plagued by legions of intra-fighting. Tribes would raid one another and in battles the Britons were intrepid as well as merciless. They employed iron weapons and leaders rode in chariots and were equipped with bronze armor and helmets.

The Britons were fond of fighting and it was these tribal battles that gave way to the Roman conquest.

Roman Britain

The Roman Annexation of Britain — 43 A.D.

In compliance with the orders of Emperor Claudius, the Roman army executed a successful invasion of Britain in 43 A.D. Though this was Rome's first prosperous capture of Britain, it surly wasn't her first attempt. A century before this annexation, in 55 and 54 B.C., Emperor Julius Caesar carried out two attempts to seize Britain. But as a result of revolt in Gaul (latter-day France) the operations failed and Julius came to a peaceful arrangement with the British people, by giving them the option to pay tribute in exchange for peace.

Then in 43 A.D. after Claudius acceded to the throne, the deserted operation of Julius resumed.

Rome was then an affluent republic with the greatest territorial expanse in the world, so it's quite evident that Britain presented little or no significance. But Claudius, as a new emperor, was being challenged by a threatening opposition from Rome's House of Lords (Senate). And so he decided to conquer Britain, make a political statement, gain advocates and secure his throne.

Claudius sent out approximately four legions of about 40,000 soldiers for the invasion of Britain. They were all under the command of Aulus Plautius. And each division had its own leader, the future emperor Vespasian being one of them.

After the arrival of the Roman army in Britain—presumably in Richborough or Chichester, or both— they went into battle with the domineering Catuvellauni tribe on the River Medway. But it wasn't long before the tribe was defeated and the Romans took control of the Southeast, forcing the tribe to flee the capital Colchester and to what is now called South Wales.

The army then advanced to the Southwest of Britain and fought a war of sieges with the western tribes to enfeeble the great Iron Age hill forts. But as they journeyed through and beyond the Midlands and approached Wales they were confronted by a resistance headed by the prince of the Catuvellauni tribe, Caratacus.

 It took the Romans decades to capture Wales.

The Foundation of London — 50 A.D

Before the arrival of the Roman Legions, London (Londinium) was a mere countryside with several streams. The Romans built a bridge across the river Thames soon after their arrival and then the history of London began.

The new conquerors were pleased by the distance and depth of the water, for it provided the virtue of serving as a bulwark against the barbarian tribes and an ideal opening for ocean going vessels. And so they decided to build a port. Then around 50 A.D. Roman merchants began to settle around the bridge. And that was when the city of London was founded.

Ten years after its foundation, however, the city of London suffered from the vicious attack of Boudicca's army and was literally turned to ashes. But its conquerors weren't deterred by this devastating incident. They knew what potential the town had and so they exerted all they had to rebuild the city. And by the 2nd century, London became the largest and most important city in Roman Britain, housing about 60,000 people and serving as one of the Empire's major commercial centers.

During this period the Romans also bordered the City with a great stone wall of about 20 feet long.

Romans Conquer Wales and the North — 70 A.D.

The Catuvellauni prince, Caratacus, who is also known as Caradoc in Welsh folklore, in alliance with the Silures tribe in Southern Wales resisted the Roman invasion for decades. But then in the Battle of Caer Caradoc in 47 A.D., a campaign operated by Publius Ostorius Scapula, Catuvellauni was defeated and later on captured by the Romans. During his trial he intrepidly asked Emperor

Claudius,"*Why do you, who have all this, wish to conquer our poor huts in Britain?*" He then declared that he would choose death than to be a slave. Owing to the courageous act he displayed, the Emperor granted him and his family pardon. He spent the rest of his life in Rome.

Despite Caratacus' fate, however, the heavy resistances of Roman rule in Wales never ceased. After Scapula's death in 52 A.D. another governor named Aulus Didius Gallus came to power and took control of the matters in Wales. He made notable strides in keeping the Welsh borders under control, but he didn't attempt to make advances to the north or west, for Claudius saw more lose than gain in the operation.

But when Nero came to power after Claudius' death in 54 A.D. a new governor, Gaius Suetonius Paulinus, was appointed to pacify the dissenters in Wales. But his campaign was promptly suspended due to the greatest uproar the Romans have ever seen in Britain – The Boudicca's Revolt.

Then years later, the Romans charged at Wales again, and this time they ended up conquering the Silures tribe. And by 77 A.D. they defeated Ordovices and brought the whole of Wales under Roman rule.

The Boudicca's Revolt — 61 A.D.

No amount of power was big enough to defeat the Roman conquerors. But Boudicca came very close to achieving what was nearly impossible— banishing them from British soil.

The Boudicca Revolt began when the Romans killed the leader of the Iceni tribe, Prasutagus, seized his property and brutally assaulted his wife, Boudicca, and her two daughters. Fueled by overpowering rage, Boudicca became the leader of the Iceni people and assembled an army of about 70,000 soldiers to avenge the Romans for their evil deeds.

Her army first advanced to Camulodunum (Colchester), a town that was guarded by just a few soldiers. Boudicca's army then took the town by storm; they looted it through and through and burned it to the ground.

The rebels then headed for Londinium (London). Upon their arrival the Roman soldiers did whatever was possible to keep them at bay, but Boudicca's huge army was relentless and unstoppable. And so they soon entered the city and raided it viciously; many pedestrians were slaughtered and the town was burned to the ground. The rebels then progressed to yet another town, Verulamium (St. Albans) and raided it as they did the others.

But then Boudicca decided to take on the Roman Army, one that was commanded by Suetonius Paulinus. The battle took place between St. Albans and Wroxeter. In this event Boudicca's army was destroyed and she managed to escape but eventually killed herself by taking poison.

The Settlement of the Anglo-Saxon in Britain — 401-410 A.D.

When the Roman Empire was under the siege of the Goths and other invaders, the Roman legions headquartered in Britain were called back to Rome to protect the kingdom. The last Roman legions left Britain in A.D. 410, leaving the Celts (Britons) open to invasion. As the Roman offshoot didn't train the Britons to fight in battles, they were pretty much exposed. Germanic tribes from north-western Europe began to raid Britain. They pillaged cattle, grain, and other valuables immediately following the Roman troops' withdrawal.

The beleaguered Celts called for help from Rome; no help arrived. The Roman Empire itself was end route to a colossal collapse so they couldn't spare any military force. The Celts were forced to face the onslaught alone.

The Picts attacked from the North, tearing down the Hardians Wall; with them came the Scots— tribes that had descended from Ireland.

The first Saxon tribes to have arrived in Britain are believed to be the Jutes; they arrived in AD 449/50. The King Vortigern of the Celts was deceived by the chief warriors of the migrationHengest and Horsa. The king proposed an offer: Land for the Saxons in exchange for their help in the battles with the Picts. Hengest and Horsa agreed and declared that they only wanted land that can encompass the hide of a bull. They lied. Once they arrived they set out to conquer England. In the Battle of Aylesford (A.D. 455) Hengest and Horsa battled against Vortigern and triumphed in a region known as Aylesford. They settled in Kent in A.D 450. In the battlefield, Horsa was slaughtered and Hengest, with his son Æsc, ascended to the throne. Together they fought three momentous and bloody battles in which they trounced the Britons. Among the wars was the Battle of Wippedesfleot (A.D. 465).

A succession of tribes from Germany flowed in and the conquest took many years. Jutes (or Frisians) settled in the extreme south-east, Kent and the Isle of Wight. The Saxons were the next to migrate to England; they settled in the south of the Thames. The last wave of immigrants was the Angles who dwelled in the central parts of the island, north of the Thames.

The Celts were supplanted and at times enslaved by the invaders. They were pushed westward to the mountainous lands (Wales and Brittany of France). They put up a brave resistance for about a century and a half until A.D. 600. King Arthur was a prominent figure at the time; he and his Knights of the Round Table advanced heroic pursuits. The Britons maintained their independence for hundreds of years in Wales. Known to the Saxons as "Foreigners", they were called "Welsh."

Kingdoms of the Picts and Scots in the north remained intact. The Celts were a majority in Scotland, Wales and Cornwall.

During the conquest of Britain, the Anglo-Saxon razed relics of the Roman Empire, the cities and the towns, churches, temples and villages. They were able to stamp their culture on the conquered society. The Latin language disappeared; Anglo-Saxon became the domineering language and from it English was born. The Britons, however, did not forsake their ancient Celtic Language.

Anglo Saxon Britain

The sources of the Anglo-Saxon period are mainly from Gildas' The Ruin of Britain (C. 540) ; Bede's Ecclesiastical History of the English People (one of the early 8th century's writings); The Anglo-Saxon Chronicle (9th century).

The Heptarchy

Heptarchy is a term employed to mention the seven kingdoms: Wessex, East Anglia, Mercia, Northumbria (includes the sub-kingdoms Bernica and Deira), Kent, Sussex and Essex.

There existed a glut of intra-fighting among the kingdoms. Eventually the larger kingdoms absorbed the smaller ones until three large ones remained: Northumbria in the north; Mercia at the center and Wessex in the south— the land of the west Saxons.

The rivalry between these three entities was fierce; at different periods, each of them assumed superior positions. Northumbria was once the supreme kingdom in A.D 617. Then in the 8th century, A.D 779, Mercia took over. Wessex gained the fore of leadership in the end, annexing all the other kingdoms. This is where the Kings and Queens of Britain hail from.

The Battle of Mount Badon — 510 A.D.

"The Battle of Badon, in which Arthur carried the Cross of our Lord Jesus Christ for three days and three nights upon his shoulders (or shield) and the Britons were the victors"—The Annals Cambriae (Annals of Wales).

A limited resource is available about the Battle of Badon (Badon Hill or the Siege of Mount Badon), but it was a battle between Celtic forces-- spearheaded by the famous King Arthur and an Anglo-Saxon troop in A.D. 510.

Although the battle failed to be mentioned in the Anglo-Saxon chronicles, it was a significant event for Medieval Britain.

The battle of Badon was fought between the Britons (Celtics) and an alliance of Kent and Sussex kingdoms led by Ælle and/or Octha, where the Britons gained a significant victory over the Anglo-Saxons, driving them back to the east and crushing their power for a century.

The Return of the Christianity through St. Augustine — 597 A.D.

Although other parts of the British Isles remained Christian, the Anglo-Saxons adhered to their pagan worship. They believed in the gods of war and nature, such as Thor, Odin and Freya.

Ireland—never invaded by the Anglo-Saxons— became the epicenter of Christianity in the region. St. Patrick in the 5th century taught and lived there. He was succeeded by St. Colombia and other Celtic missionaries a hundred years later. They spread the teachings of Jesus to the Scots, Picts and the Angles at the north.

But it took Pope Gregory the Great and his initiative to penetrate through the Anglo-Saxons. He sent his friend St. Augustine, who was a leader of a monastery in Rome, with twelve monks for the quest of converting the Anglo-Saxon. Ironically, St. Augustine and his monks landed in Kent in AD 597— the very spot where a hundred years ago Hengest and Horsa had arrived.

The king of Kent, Ethelbert, gave Augustine and his compatriots consent to pursue their mission in Canterbury where the relics of an old Roman Christian Church existed. The church was rebuilt and a monastery along with a Christian school was built. Augustine became the earliest Archbishop of Canterbury.

Shortly after, King Ethelbert, whose wife was already a Christian, was converted to a catholic. This led to the Canterbury monks and Celtic missionaries reaching out to all parts of Britain. During the 7th century the whole of Britain was converted to Christianity. Monasteries and churches were established around the country.

The reintroduction of Christianity to Britain brought back the practice of reading and writing books; with this emerged an educated caste literate in Latin; civilization of the society also took root then.

The literate men, priests and monks provided council to the kingdoms of the land on government matters.

Thirty years later King Wodwin of Northumbria was converted by missionary called Paulinus.

The fact that all the kingdoms believed in one religion and acknowledged one religious authority of the Archbishop of Canterbury and the pope helped unite Britain later on in the years.

The Northumbrian Supremacy — 617 A.D.

The Anglian kingdom of Northumbria (654-954) was situated in what is today north England and south-east England. It was founded in the early 7th century by Æthelfirth— the king of Bernicia who later annexed Deira in A.D. 604 to create Northumbria's kingdom.

An element of the heptarchy, Northumbria reached its peak in A.D. 617 with its reign extending from the south of Humber to the River Mersey. Those territories are today's— north-east England, Yorkshire and the Humber, north-west England (Cumbria included), and the Scottish boarders Edinburgh, East Lothian, West Lothian and Midlothian.

In its decline, the kingdom lost its southern territory (former Deira) to the Danelaw. The kingdom managed to retain power of its northern territory (former Bernicia) but it was eventually ceded to an earldom by the Danish kingdom which had deemed it peripheral.

The Mercian Supremacy —626-821 A.D.

The genesis of the kingdom of Mercia is still a rather vague topic, but its capital was the town of Tamworth. This location was established by King Creoda in A.D. 534. It has since served as the seat of all Mercian kings.

The Mercian kingdom enjoyed supremacy over the six kingdoms (Essex, Kent, Sussex, East Anglia and Wessex) for nearly two hundred years from the 7th century to the 8th century. It either annexed the other kingdoms as a territory or acquired their submission.

Mercia became the dominant kingdom in Britain south of the River Humber. This epoch is called the "Mercian supremacy". It is, moreover, known as the "Golden Age of Mercia" because of King Offa's Dyke which marked the Welsh and Mercian kingdom borders.

The kingdom's collapse commenced at the end of the 9th century after the invasion of the Vikings who had annexed most of the Mercian territories into the Danelaw.

The last of the Mercian kings was Ceolwulf II who died in A.D.879—this was the same time when the kingdom lost all autonomy. It was later governed by an earldom who answered to the king of Wessex "Alfred the Great" otherwise known as the King of the Anglo-Saxon.

Viking Britain

First Invasion by the Vikings — 793 A.D.

The first recorded Vikings raid in Britain was in A.D. 793 at the largely unfortified monastic site in Lindisfarne. The callous Vikings ransacked the area slewing several monks and carried out extensive raids regularly around England's coasts. They pillaged treasures and goods of other kinds, and imprisoned people to enslave them. Targeted areas often included monasteries due to their precious gold chalices, plates, crucifixes, bowls and silver. Though the first violent units were small, it is believed that the raid had been carried out strategically.

The raiding signaled the beginning of the 'Viking Age of Invasion.'

Progressively, the Viking began to settle. They first settled in winter camps, then in soils they captured, largely in the eastern and northern parts of England.

The Viking raid did not cease over the years. Various kinds of Viking groups made frequent trips to Britain's coast for over three-hundred years following A.D. 793.

The Great Danish Army Invades Britain — 866-877 A.D.

The Vikings who invaded England were Danes from Denmark in the 9th century. They began with a series of attacks on the east coast of England in 835, destroying churches, abbeys, monasteries and other buildings while seizing treasures.

The great armies conquered the kingdoms of East Anglia, Northumbria, and some areas of Mercia; only the kingdom of Wessex put out a strong resistance but it eventually came under their invasion. Modern York (Jorvik) was captured by the Vikings in 866. This was their capital city.

They decided to settle permanently in England, given that the resistance against them was ill-organized. This was the first step in the establishment of the Danelaw which was located in eastern and north-eastern England of the time. It was governed by the Danish. The Danes who remained in England were lastly assimilated into the English population.

England's Viking conquest came to an end in 1066. This happened when Harald Hardrada, with his men, went to Stamford Bridge. The king of England, Harold Godwinson, together with his unit, marched to the north and overpowered Hardrada in the extended and bloodstained battle. England repelled the final invasion of Scandinavia.

King Harold, following the exhausting battle, heard right away that another invading troop arrived in Kent which was led by William of Normandy. Without having to rest, King Harold's army marched quickly back to the south to meet with this new threat. The worn out English army battled the Normans at the Battle of Hastings on 14th October, 1066. This was the time where King Harold died, and William was crowned king of England.

William was a descendent of the Vikings. Rollo, his great-great-great grandfather, was a Viking. He, in A.D. 911, conquered Normandy in the north part of France. His people eventually became French. The last achieved raid of England, however, was in a way another Viking one.

King Alfred Defeats the Vikings — 871 A.D.

The king who managed to save Wessex and England from the Danish Army was the most celebrated English king in the Anglo-Saxon times— Alfred the Great. He was born in Wantage in A.D. 849. By A.D. 871, King Alfred engaged in the war against the Danes.

Alfred waged war against the 'Grand Army' of the Danes for 15 years, maintaining the freedom of Wessex from Viking influence. The Anglo-Saxon Chronicle illustrates in details the vicissitudes of the military struggle with the

Danes, particularly in the section known as the Parker Manuscript.

Alfred succeeded in leading out his organized army against the Vikings after covertly gathering his dispersed army while he was hiding in the woods and marshes near Athelney (Somerset). And in A.D. 878 he completely triumphed over the Great Heathen Army led by Guthrum at the Battle of Edington. Guthrum, the Viking leader, following the battle, changed to Christianity.

The same year a treaty created by Alfred the Great, Treaty of Wedmore, was signed with Guthrum, bestowing the Vikings territory known as the Danelaw. It consisted of the north-east, north-west and eastern parts of England, while Alfred and his successors controlled Wessex. People in Danelaw had to abide by the Danish rule.

Conquest was no longer pondered by the Danes, and they began to settle as farmers and integrated with the English. (During the reigns of Alfred's son and grandson the Danelaw became reunited with the rest of England.)

In later years, Alfred began to reconstruct areas that the Vikings ransacked, restored damaged churches and monasteries.

He believed that a king's onus was not merely safeguarding his people but also providing them education and good governance. In his reign, the first history in

English language was commenced— "The Anglo-Saxon Chronicle."

King Alfred gained popularity across Europe, not only for overpowering the Danes but for also being a sagacious ruler. He is called the founder of the English navy because he established the first great galleys with which the English were able to obliterate several Viking ships.

Athelstan, Alfred's grandson, became England's first actual King. In A.D. 937, he defeated the Vikings at the Battle of Brunaburh, and managed to include the Danelaw in his newly born kingdom.

The Commencement of the Anglo-Saxon Chronicle — 890 A.D.

The Anglo-Saxon Chronicle is the earliest known recording of England's history that has been written in English. Historians believe that the creation of the first script of the Anglo-Saxon Chronicle dates back to ruling days of Alfred the Great, in A.D. 890. Multiple copies of that single original chronicle was produced and then dispersed to monasteries across England. Revisions and updates of this chronicle subsisted up until 1154. It was first written in old English (Anglo-Saxon), but later records were probably written in Middle English.

The Anglo-Saxon Chronicle is believed to be the oldest history of any European country in a vernacular language.

The Chronicle lasted until the modern period in seven manuscripts from nine (in the 18th century one of these were destroyed). Seven of these nine manuscripts and remains today are housed in the British Library. The other two are located in Oxford and Parker Library of Corpus Christi College, at Bodleian Library.

The Winchester (Parker) Chronicle is the oldest surviving document of the *Chronicle*. It began at the Old Minster, Winchester, near the end of Alfred's reign. The document commences with the pedigree of Alfred.

King Canute of Denmark Becomes King of England — 1016 A.D.

Canute, as a lad, followed his father in the invasion of England in A.D. 1013. After seeing how weak "King Ethelred the Unready" or "the Unwise" was, the Danes began their invasion and King Sweyn of Denmark overpowered Ethelred and compelled him to flee to Normandy; however, Sweyn himself died in the hour of victory. Harald, Canute's brother, became Sweyn's successor and claimed the kingship of Denmark. The English then requested for their king Ethelred, who had ran off during the invasion of Sweyn, to return to England and his throne.

To amass his forces, Canute headed back to Denmark. Then around 1015 he resumed his campaign against

Ethelred's army. Canute managed to defeat all forces and annex almost all of England, except for London. The English Witan (or council), around Ethelred's demise, appointed Canute as King of England; London, however, selected Edmund Ironside, Ethelred's son.

There were quite a lot of battles in which Canute and Edmund fought. But after Canute won a conspicuous victory in October 1016 at Ashingdon, Edmund comprised on dividing the kingdom. Then around the end of the month November, Canute came across some luck when Edmund died and he became the sole ruler of England as a whole.

Initially, Canute employed austere measures: he ordered the killing of influential English adversaries, arranged the assassination of Edmund Ironside's brother, and even forced Edmund's family to flee and seek refuge in Hungary. In time, however, he started to adopt a rather equitable policy, which allowed the way for more Englishmen to rise to power.

He ruled astutely and his reign demonstrated stability, tranquility, and success.

Medieval Britain

The Battle of Hastings — 1066

On October 14th, 1066 two forces stood opposite each other: the English army of King Harold II in one line; the forces of William of Normandy in another. They fought all day near Hastings on the south coast of England. Following the conclusion of the battle Harold was murdered and his armies were destroyed. There are two accounts in regards to what brought about his death; one is that he was killed by the shot of an arrow in the eye, and the other, the terrible slash of a sword. Harold was England's last Anglo-Saxon king.

According to Norman historians, the duke of Normandy, William, is said to have went to England to visit his cousin and the king of England, Edward the Confessor, just two week before he raided England and claimed the English Throne.

It is believed that during this visit Edward pledged to make William the rightful successor to the English throne. On his deathbed, however, Edward had a change of heart and made Harold Godwin his heir.

In January 1066, King Edward passed away and Harold Godwin was appointed King Harold II. Quickly, William debated his claim.

September, 1066, William arrived in England .sey, with an army of 7,000 and cavalry. He then .aled his army to Hastings and spent some time .anizing his forces. And on the 13th October, Harold .vith his army landed not far from Hastings. At around 9:00am, the following day, William led his army out to launch the battle.

Soon after William triumphed at the Battle of Hastings; he marched to London and obtained the city's compliance. On the 25th of December 1066, in Westminster Abbey, he was ushered in and proclaimed to be the first Norman king of England. This event marked the end of the Anglo-Saxon phase in England's history. The language that became employed in the King's court was French. Then it gradually blended with the Anglo-Saxon language till it evolved into modern English.

Magna Carta — 1215

To none will we sell, to none will we deny, right or justice.

An excerpt from the charter

Magna Carta was the first charter in England's history that declared the liberty of the English man. In June 12th,1215 the barons of Britain made King John (1199-1216) sign the celebrated Magna Carta at Runnymede, which limited his arbitrary power, prohibiting him from collecting unconstitutional taxes and taking punitive measures against any free man, unlawfully.

This was a telling event that made the king understand that he too was under the law.

The Magna Carta served as a bulwark against the misuse of authority.

The signing of Magna Carta allowed the baron the power to check the work of the government. During the feudal days the barons would provide counseling to the kings on governmental matters. And royal officers and sheriffs were selected from this caste.

The signing of this great charter exhibited the strength of the baron class in Britain, but more importantly it serves as a relic of humanity's assertion of liberty.

The Hundred Years War with France — 1337-1453

Feudalism was the kind of system that bathed the Lords and nobles with wealth and power and enfeebled the Kingdom. But in England, during the reign of William I, Henry I, and Henry II, feudalism was corroded a great deal, giving the kingdom more power and control over the country.

In France, on the other hand, the Feudal system was still at its peak, and the king had little or no control over his nobles.

The Hundred Years War began when Edward III decided to attack France in 1337. Almost all of his soldiers were freemen who were recruited and had a handsome pay for their service. And the French king was left with no other choice but to depend on the feudal lords and their forty day's military service. So Edward knew all was in his favor. And to validate his stand, his army conquered the French nobles and their followers without let or hindrance on their first attack.

Then for the next hundred years, the intermittent warfare between the two nations continued.

The British army won most of the battles; the battles of Crecy (1346), Poitiers (1356), and Agincourt (1415) were amongst the most famous combats. As a result of these victories, the British were able to succeed in conquering a large part of France.

The return of the British soldiers was part of what made this war all the more popular in England, as they came back affluent from the plunders of French towns and villages. And the parliament, seeing the profitability of the war, frequently supported its continuance.

Edward III recruited more soldiers and issued an order for every free man to practice shooting the longbow and learn how to be a good soldier.

Near the end, the French began to change their techniques. Instead of fighting in big battles, in which they were quite ill-fated, they began to use their armies to besiege the castles built by the English to guard their conquests.

The war came to an end in 1453.

The Hundred Years War was regarded as England's greatest blessing, for it was what gave the entire nation self-respect and pride in their own race and language.

The Black Death — 1348

"Wretched, terrible, destructive year, the remnants of the people alone remains," reads a carved inscription at St. Mary's, Ashwell, Hertfordshire.

The Black Death, otherwise known as the bubonic plague claimed the lives of millions of people in Medieval England between 1348 and 1350.

This ruthlessly pervasive plague took London by storm in September 1348. It then quickly spread all along the coast of East Anglia.

Wales and Midlands were hit in the spring of 1349. And by the end of the summer it traveled beyond the Irish Sea and pervaded the North with its deadly spell. And Scotland was plagued by the Black Death a little latter, in 1350. Ironically, the Scotts would have evaded the attack of the plague had they not taken the opportunist attempt to invade England after hearing of their turmoil.

"The Scots, hearing of the cruel plague of the English, declared that it had befallen them through the revenging hand of God, and they took to swearing by 'the foul death of England' - or so the common report resounded in the ears of the English. And thus the Scots, believing that the English were overwhelmed by the terrible vengeance of God, gathered in the forest of Selkirk with the intention of invading the whole realm of England. The fierce mortality came upon them, and the sudden cruelty of a monstrous death winnowed the Scots. Within a short space of time, around 5000 of them had died, and the rest, weak and strong alike, decided to retreat to their own country"
Henry Knighton

The plague is believed to have been brought from Asia in late 1348 through trading ships at the Sicilian port of Messing. And evidence showed that the epidemic did spread through most parts of Europe during that century, but none were as severely affected by it as that of the populace in England.

The lack of medical knowledge obviously played a major role in exacerbating the plague. But the ill-conducted disposal of the bodies, the unsanitary condition in which the majority of the serfs lived, and the mobilization of goods and people during warfare's, was also part of what helped the spread.

Many believed that the Bubonic plague was the divine punishment from God. And so for mercy some would publicly flog themselves with heavy leather straps studded with sharp pieces of metal. This was a ritual most would repeat three times a day.

The War of the Roses — 1455-1485

The Wars of the Roses came just two years after the conclusion of the Hundred Years War.

The Wars of the Roses in England was a series of battles between the House of York and the House of Lancaster. Each side brandished roses to represent itself; the Lancastrian had red rose and the Yorkists, white rose, hence the name of this civil war 'The Wars of the Roses.'

It was a conglomerate of disagreements that brought about this destructive civil war. Both parties, having decedents of Edward III, claimed rights to the throne. And when the

Lancastrian King Henry VI came to power in 1422 and proved to have a weak and unjust rule over the country, the Yorkists rebelled and began to pursue the throne.

Henry VI was at the time battling mental problems. And as he lapsed into insanity in 1454, the Yorkists took the opportunity and made it possible for Richard, the duke of York, to be titled the 'protector of the realm.'

But Henry VI recovered shortly, in 1455. And his reestablishment of authority and punitive pursuit of the Yorkisits lead to the outbreak of the civil war.

On May 22nd 1455, the first battle of the wars took place at St. Albans, in which the Yorkists came out the victors.

This war was succeeded by a legion of battles between the Lancastrians and Yorkists.

The Yorkists triumphed in most of these battles. And ultimately the 'Duke of York' was proclaimed King Edward IV at Westminster on March 4th, 1461; he died in 1483 with his title.

During this war Henry VI along with his wife Margaret of Anjou and their son were left with no other choice but to seek refuge in Scotland. But they soon returned back to England with their army, in an attempt to reclaim the throne. But Edward IV defeated their army and their attempt came to a miserable fall. In this event, Henry VI was killed in the Tower of London, Margaret was arrested and their son was killed.

Tudor Britain

The Termination of the War of the Roses — 1485

The death of the Yorkist king Edward IV in 1483 was what initially marked the beginning of the War's end. After his death, Richard III, Edward's brother, claimed the throne by outstripping his nephew, Edward V.

In this instance, many Yorkists, who were scandalized by this arrangement, were subjected to alienation. And they eventually decided to turn to the last remaining Lancastrian hope, Henry Tudor, the founder of the House of Tudor and who was later known as Henry VII.

Then in 1485, Henry VII, with the sound support of the French and the dissenting Yorkists, was able to defeat and kill Richard III at Bosworth Field.

And by marrying Edward's daughter, Elizabeth, Henry had the ability to unite the Lancastrians and Yorkists, and terminate the age-old feud of the Wars of the Roses, in 1486.

Henry VIII Becomes King of England — 1509

Henry VIII was born on June 28th, 1491, at the Greenwich Palace in England. He was the second son of King Henry VII and Elizabeth of York.

After the sudden death of the initial heir, Henry's elder brother Arthur, he became the immediate successor of the throne. And soon after his father's passing in 1509, he claimed his title and became King Henry VIII.

He was fifteen years of age when he acceded to power. So during his first years in rule he relied heavily on Thomas Wolsey, who by 1515 was made Lord Chancellor, the highest rank in government, for his loyalty and service.

In regards to military achievements Henry was most acclaimed for the remarkable advancements of the British Navy. He built approximately 50 naval ships and installed latest guns on several vessels, one of which being the Mary Rose, during his reign; need be mentioned, that there were only five Royal Warships when he first came to power.

Henry was also the one who built the first naval dock in Britain at Portsmouth and the Navy Board in 1546. For these accomplishments he was known as the 'Father of Royal Navy.'

Henry VIII was a king who led a rather bohemian personal life, one that is of an endless stream of stories – his six marriages and their disastrous end being the most famous.

His first marriage was to his deceased brother's widow, Catherine of Aragon, a union for which he obtained the papal dispensation. Catherin gave birth to six children, but only one survived and that was the future queen Mary I.

His second marriage was to Anne Boleyn, Catherine's lady-in-waiting, and the sister of his other mistress. She gave birth to Elizabeth (the future Queen Elizabeth I). And in his third marriage to Jane Seymour, Henry fathered his successor Edward VI.

Anne of Cleves, Catherine Howard, and Catherine Parr were the remaining three.

Henry VIII died on January 28th, 1547, and was buried in St. George's Chapel at Windsor Castle, next to Jane Seymour.

The Formation of the Church of England — 1534

The separation of the Church of England from the Roman Catholic Church was yet another one of Henry VIII's telling deeds.

This part of Britain's history began when Henry fell madly in love with Anne Boleyn and sought out an annulment for his marriage from his first wife Catherine of Aragon from Pope Clement VII.

His appeal to Pope Clement VII, which was presented by Henry's most devout and trusted Cardinal Wolsey was rejected. Wolsey argued that the union was only legal by the grace of a papal dispensation, which was indeed a solid reason, but Clement VII wasn't keen on reversing the decision of a predecessor or opposing Emperor Charles V, who supported Queen Catherine, his aunt. And so Wolsey was left with no other choice but to return to his king with the rejection.

As a result of this failure, Wolsey was dismissed from his position and arrested on the trumped up count of treason.

With exhausted patience, Henry then decided to take matters in to his own hands. He persuaded the parliament to pass measures that denied the authority of the Pope and ended up establishing the Church of England, making himself the church's ecclesiastical head.

As a result of this reformation Catholics who kept affirming papal supremacy were beheaded; Protestants who opposed a single Catholic dogma were burnt at the stake, and thousands who failed to comply with these two regulations were killed.

Another punitive measure that Henry took against the Catholic Church, though this decision of his was relatively based on economical purposes, was the suppression and confiscation of the monasteries' lands and properties.

Henry's decision to break away from Rome had nothing to do with religion. He was indeed a devout Catholic, so much so that even the pope awarded him the title 'Defender of the Faith' after he publicly denounced the Lutheran doctrine in his book 'Assertio Septem Sacramentorum.'

And despite his feud and separation with Rome, he remained a devout Catholic till the day he died, and never did he allow the protestant ideology to pervade the English church. That is of course until his son and successor, Edward VI acceded to power.

The Union of Wales and England — 1536

After the annexation of Wales by King Edward I of England in 1282, Wales became part of England. However, the nations were legally bound after the signing of the Act of Union in 1536-1542.

Henry VIII's decision to break the cord that tied England to the Church of Rome declared the nations independence. And to strengthen this sovereignty, he felt the importance of abolishing the Lords of the March in Wales, which were then divided into seven counties, Flint, Denbigh, Montgomery, Brecon, Radnor, Monmouth, Pembroke, and Glamorgan.

Henry's government enacted the Act of Union in 1536. It was written in about 7,500 words and it stated that the law of England was to be the only law of Wales. And that, for administrative purposes, there will be Justices of the peace chaired in every county. The treaty also stated that Wales was to be represented in parliament by 26 members.

The most controversial segment of this statute was the section that dealt with the Welsh language. It stated that the only language in the courts of Wales was to be English. But as the majority of the populace in Wales had Welsh as their first and only language, this legislation was short lived and translators were heavily used in the courts.

The act brought, for the first time in Wales' history, uniformity in the administration of Justice in every county. And as a result of further reformation of the act in 1543, Welsh MPs increased to 27 and the council of Wales at Ludlow and the Marches were given statutory recognition, which allowed them to employ jurisdiction over Wales and the four border counties of England.

The Formation of the East India Company — 1600

The Tudors were smart leaders that have played an enormous role in the making of Britain's history. And one of their great accomplishments was the establishment of the English East India Company, by the last remaining Tudor (Elizabeth I).

The formation of this company began when a set of merchants convened and outlined a plan to cruise to the Indian Ocean and have a hand in the prolific spice importation business. Two years later, they convened again, and this time with the capital to fund their endeavor and determination to seek out the Queen's approval and support for the project.

Then on December 31st 1600, under the title "Governor and Company of Merchants of London Trading with the East Indies" Queen Elizabeth I approved a Royal Charter to Earl of Cumberland, George, 215 knights, Aldermen and Burgeses.

This charter paved the way for this newfound company to have superior control on trade with the countries in the west of the Straits of Magellan and East of the Cape of Good Hope, for the following fifteen years.

The company's first sail was in 1601 and it returned to England in 1603; it was commanded by Sir James Lancaster. During this period the company established a factory in Java. Then two years later, another factory was established on the coast of Bay of Bengal in Machilipatnam. All of the company's ships arrived at Sural, a dock established in 1608 as a trade transit route.

Despite its many prosperous journeys though, the East India Company still had to battle out the grave dangers posed by its rivals, the Dutch in the Dutch East Indies (now Indonesia) and the Portuguese. So the company clearly had to accouter itself for all safety reasons. But this insignificant defense system grew to becoming a power that's to be reckoned with.

This quasi-military power the East India Company developed, didn't only guarantee its safety, but it also gave the company the power to rule. By establishing its own administrative department and exercising its military power, which was composed of about 67,000 soldiers, the company literally became an imperial power and eventually had complete control over large areas in India.

But after the British Crown colonized India in 1858, the corporation began to gradually dissolve, both commercially and politically. Then by 1873 the East India Company came to an end, when the Colonial Office absorbed its armies and all its governmental functions.

Stuart Britain

The period from the 17th century to the 18th century—commonly known as the Age of the Absolute Monarchy—was a tumultuous era for Britain. As most of Europe acquiesced in absolute monarchy, Britain revolted and established the world's first constitutional monarchy.

James VI of Scotland and the I of England — 1603

In A.D 1536, James (1566-1625) and Elizabeth I were bound by an alliance under the Treaty of Berwick. His mother Mary, Queen of Scots, was executed by Elizabeth the next year. James veiled his apathy with a feign protest—his eye was feasted on the ascension to the throne of England. And in 1603 James VI of Scotland was crowned James I of England following the passing away of Elizabeth I—the last Tudor. He united the two kingdoms of Scotland and England.

John I ruled by divine right and brooked little dissent. He was quite unpopular and his notoriety emanated from his abuse of his prerogatives, extravaganza and his persistent coercion of parliament to stretch his financial allowances.

James' greatest achievement would be the translation of the Bible (The Authorized Version) which still is used in Britain today.

The Gun Powder Plot— 1605

James was a thorn to the Catholics who he had coerced to attend protestant churches. As retaliation a cell of Catholics pursued an unsuccessful attempt to blow the House of Parliament at the presence of James I on the 5th November, 1605. This was called the Gun Powder Plot. The plan was thwarted; one of the groups called Guy Fawkes was caught and burnt at the stake. Annually, the failure of the Gun Powder Plot was celebrated on November 5th. As an emblem, a pageantry of firework would be displayed and a straw man (called Guy) would be set alight.

Charles I

James' successor and son Charles I was equally unpopular, if not more. He inherited his father's penchant to assert the divine right. Exacerbating his odium was his marriage to the catholic Henrietta Maria—sister of Louis XIII. Charles made a secret oath to bestow British Catholics exclusive privileges; this devotion bode ill to his reign.

Charles I argued with the parliament on matters of taxes and religion. Composed of many puritans, the parliament wished for Britain to forsake the formalities of bishops and ceremonies in worship and wanted to create a simpler form of religion. Charles wasn't welcoming to the idea and pursued a very oppressive regime towards the puritans. In 1620, some puritans known as the Pilgrim Fathers set out to America to build a new life and to liberally follow their faith.

The relationship between the parliament and Charles continued to sour and he dissolved the parliament. He ruled England alone for a decade—this period is known as the Personal Rule of Charles.

Charles continued with his crusade of installing the catholic religion in the nation. He continued to oppress and suppress puritans and reintroduced catholic practices and dogmas into the Anglican Church. He also persisted to establish religious uniformity as well.

When he attempted to establish the same radical regulations in Scotland, demanding the bishops govern the Scottish Church (the Presbyterian Church), he ignited a rebellion. The Scotts deposed the King's bishop and organized an army to attack England; after that followed the battle known as the Bishops War.

In 1639 Charles marched to the Scottish lands with his forces to quell the uprising; however, an inconclusive military collision led to a truce proposed by the Scots—the Pacification of Berwick.

Charles, bent on ending the rebellion, needed money so he called parliament again in 1640. This didn't accomplish much since Charles dismissed the parliament in a few weeks –thus the name the 'Short Parliament'—when opposition rose against the invasion of Scotland.

Going against the parliament's advice, Charles broke the truce and attacked Scotland. This round, the Scotts not only managed to defeat his army but occupied nearly the entire northern region of England. He was even cowed into paying a large sum of £850 a day to the Scotts lest they forge ahead in their invasion.

Beleaguered by a massive political and financial dilemma, Charles I had no other choice but to resort to summoning another English parliament. This Parliament—known as the Long Parliament— was even more hostile towards him than the earlier ones. The schism between the two parties prodded the eruption of the English Civil War.

1651 English Civil War — 1642

The English Civil War was a result of a succession of battles which can be easily cataloged into three:

First war (1642-1646): the warring parties were the Royalists (Cavaliers) who were the sympathizers of

Charles I and the Parliamentarians (Roundheads). This culminated to the imprisonment of Charles I.

The Second war (between 1648 and 1649): the warring parties were the same; it was the continuation of the first war. It was ended by the beheading of Charles I.

The Third and Final civil war (1649-1651): the battle was between the acolytes of Charles II and the stout advocates of the Rump Parliament. Charles was put to exile and the parliament was the victor in this war.

England was left without a monarchy, governed first by the Common Wealth of England and later by the Protectorate (1653-1659) under Oliver Cromwell's personal rule.

The Introduction of Tea in Britain —1652-1654

It was between the years of 1652 and 1654 the first samples of tea arrived in Britain. Prior to the advent of tea there were two main meals known to the populace: breakfast, which incorporated ale, bread and beef, and dinner, which consisted of a long massive meal at the end of the day.

Tea, however, managed to gain quick popularity, enough to replace ale as the national drink. The tradition of tea drinking became the social culture.

Moreover, King Charles II, while in exile, got married to Catherine de Braganza (Catherine of Braganza) in 1662. He and his wife were known as tea drinkers. After the monarchy was restored they both imported the tea drinking tradition in Britain.

The Great Fire of London — 1666

On Sunday, September 2nd, 1666, the Great Fire of London was ignited in the baker's shop of Thomas Farynor. Situated in Pudding Lane, the bakery was incinerated and the fire quickly swept through London.

So many factors aided the rapid spread of the fire: a strong wind from the east, a city rife with timber buildings so compactly built, and scarcity of water following a severe drought that struck London earlier.

The fire was able to inflict a seismic destruction; it blazed from Pudding Lane to Thames where it reached a warehouse stacked with combustible products such as oil and tallow. Fortunately, the fire was prohibited from spreading further south of the river because a section of the London Bridge was destroyed earlier in 1633. It took the help of the Navy—there were no fire brigades then— to take out the fire which took place on Wednesday, September 5th 1666.

Although human casualties were known to officially be four, the fire annihilated 373 acres of London—from the Tower in the East to Fleet Street and Fetter Lane on the west side. 84 churches, 13,200 houses and 44 company halls were destroyed.

The fire cost London £10,000— the annual income of the city then was £12,000. London has to entirely be rebuilt. Temporary buildings were erected; they were poorly established and fueled the spread of disease. They also failed to protect the people from the harsh winter that came in the wake of the fire. Many died because of these conditions.

Society plunged into a financial chaos; the debtor's prison was congested.

It took thirty years to rebuild the city.

The Great Revolution — 1688

The monarchy was reinstalled in 1660. Charles II was called back to England by the people.

He and his son James II gave their oath to respect constitutional privileges and not to manipulate or interfere in religious policies. However, father and son—both sympathizers of the catholic religion— would come up against the parliament.

The ascension of James II to the throne was a contentious matter due to the concerns over his conversion to Catholicism. Parliament was split into two: the Whigs (opposing his crowning) and the Tories (supporting his ascension). The Tories triumphed and James II became king of England.

He incurred a great deal of opposition when he married a catholic woman who bore him a son. This was after the birth of his two protestant daughters. Being anti-catholic, England feared the prospect of a Catholic king. So Mary, James' oldest daughter, who was an Anglican and also the wife of William the Orange was invited in 1688 to take the throne in order "to save the liberties and religion of England." They both accepted and James II, after the fall of the Jacobite uprising, fled to France.

Parliament wanted to secure the "liberties and religion of England" so on December 16th, 1669 they made William and Mary sign The Bill of Rights. This is the most historic document of England. It served as bulwark against the encroachment of Parliament's right by the monarchy, limited the arbitrary power of the monarchy, insured the free election of parliament members and much besides. It also mentioned the Magna Carta.

Moreover, the Bill of Rights regulated the passing of the throne and stipulated the sovereign belong to the Anglican Church.

In 1702, by the provision of the Bill of Rights, the throne went from William and Mary to her sister Anne. And through the Act of Settlement the crown went to Anne's cousin George I (1714-1727).

On 1st May, 1707 the Act of Union was passed by the English and Scottish parliament thereby creating the United Kingdom of Great Britain.

Georgian Britain

In this epoch Britain completely departed from its medieval past and emerged as a strong nation where commercial trade and wealth became prominent. Power shifted from the Monarchy to the parliament.

The Gregorian era left a legacy of Gregorian literature and architecture. Great politicians like Sir Robert Walpole and William Pitt emerged; the industrial and agricultural revolution changed Britain phenomenally; advances in science, engineering and design were made; trade and consumerism blossomed; cities grew—this was indeed a prosperous year for Britain.

".....we are the most diligent nation in the world. Vast trade, rich manufactures, mighty wealth, universalcorrespondence, and happy success have been constant companions of England, and given us the title of an industrious people."
Daniel Defoe vaunted.

But it wasn't all glorious. Alongside the extreme luxury there existed an extreme and gnawing poverty; working conditions were also terrible.

Poverty of course is no disgrace but it is damned annoying.

William Pitt

Great Britain Appoints the First Prime Minister — 1721

After the United Kingdom of Great Britain came into being, the parliament of England and the parliament Scotland of united. Scotland sent 45 members to join existing members of England in the new House of Commons of Great Britain, and 16 representative peers to be part of the new House of Lords.

When George I ascended to the throne in October 1714 he dismissed the Tory Cabinet and supplanted it with a cabinet dominated by the Whigs. This was mainly due to the support of the Whigs to secure his crowning.

George I resented the Tories because of their earlier support for the crowning of James II and their alleged collusion with the Jacobite rebellion.

The British General Election was held in 1715 where members were recalled to serve the 5th parliament of Great Britain. The Whigs were the victors, winning a massive majority of seats in the House of Commons. Eventually the purging of the Tories in every element of government was pursued, making the Whigs a dominant figure of politics for the following fifty years.

Sir Robert Walpole (1676-1745) was elected Britain's first Prime Minister. He was a domineering political figure during the reigns of George I and George II.

The American Declaration of Independence — 1776

The period between 1700 and 1850, Britain engaged in 137 wars and uprisings. The nation came out of these mayhems successfully except in the American War of Independence (1775-1783).

Britain had just come out of the Seven Years War (1756-1763), known to Americans as the French Indian War. The warring parties were Britain, Prussia and Hanover against Austria, Saxony, Russia, France and Spain. For France and Britain, it was the rivalry for overseas supremacy. The war was concluded by the Treaty of Paris 1763 in which Britain emerged as a supreme European colonial and naval power. France ceded its territories in North America and other places to Britain.

Britain believed the American colonies needed to financially participate in the defense that British forces provided and began to levy taxes. This eventually aroused indignation among the thirteen colonies.

The first major opposition of the Americans was ignited by the Stamp Act of 1765. It was a taxation measure purposed to increase revenues for the British Army stationed in America. In protest to this legislation colonist convened the Stamp Act Congress in October 1765 under the heading "no taxation without representation."

Following months of slightly violent and strategic oppositions, the legislation was lifted and peace was restored but not for very long.

In an attempt to salvage the collapsing British East India Company, the British parliament enacted the Tea Act Bill in 1773. It imposed the lowering of the company's tea taxes and granted the corporation a monopoly over America's tea trade. This brought about the Boston Tea Party 1773.

The British responded with a punitive act of shutting down the Boston Port in Massachusetts. This act was met with fierce resistance. A coalition of twelve American colonies was established in support of the Massachusetts; they formed the Continental Congress and in April 1775 an armed conflict broke out between British forces (and their sympathizers) and the Massachusetts militias at Lexington and Concord.

The Continental Congress declared independence from Britain in July 1st, 1776. The American War of Independence was thus officially commenced.

The final and decisive combat of the war was the battle of Yorktown in 1761; Americans triumphed with the significant help of the French forces. The Treaty of Paris was signed in 1783 and the United States of America formally became an sovereign nation.

A huge blow this was to Britain, as America was the most populous colony. It brought about the shift of focus from the Americas to the Pacific, Asia and Africa.

Act of Union — 1800

The Acts of Union of 1800 is sometimes referenced as the Act of Union of 1801. It untied the kingdom of Great Britain and the kingdom of Ireland, thereby forming the United Kingdom of Great Britain and Ireland.

The Irish Rebellion of 1798 had the question of Ireland obtrude itself on British politicians. The French Revolution which had inspired the Irish Rebellion was a constant thorn to Britain. Furthermore the situation was intensified by the specter of Ireland adopting the Catholic Emancipation which would eventually have the Roman Catholic Parliament separate it from Britain and side with the French.

William Pitt the Younger (successor of Sir Robert Walpole) resolved that a union was the most fitted solution for the state of affairs.

The Slave Trade Act — 1807

The Slave Trade Act of 1807 otherwise known as the Abolition of the Slave Trade Act 1807 was introduced to the parliament of the United Kingdom of Great Britain on 10th February, 1807 and gained Royal Assent on March 25th.

It was a block of Quakers and Evangelical English Protestants that established the Committee for the Abolition of the Slave Trade in 1787. The group believed that slavery was an amoral entity that needed to be stopped. The committee acquired parliamentary factions in 1807.

The legislation put an end to the slave trade in the British Empire; however, it did not stop slavery. It wasn't until twenty years later that slavery was abolished.

The Act put immense pressure on those who opted to continue the practice. Captains who had slaves hidden in their ships would pay fines of £100 per slave.

In 1807 the Royal Navy erected the West Africa Squadron to curtail the slave trade at the coast of West Africa. The unit managed to free 150,000 slaves between 1808 and 1860.

Britain's pursuit to abolish the slave trade was exported, putting immense pressure on other European nations and the United States of America.

The Battle of Waterloo — 1815

Napoleon Bonaparte (1769-1821) had become a predominant figure in Europe in the 19th century. He rose to a high-ranking military figure during the French Revolution (1789-1799), toppled the French government in 1799 and crowned himself Emperor in 1804—there was nothing standing in between Napoleon and his lofty ambitions.

He aspired to achieve European hegemony with him at the helm. Through a legion of wars he stretched his territory across western and central Europe. But his unsuccessful and disastrous invasion of Russia among other things eventuated to the abdication of his throne and exile in 1814 to Elba— a Mediterranean Island off the coast of Italy.

Napoleon escaped from Elba on February 26th, 1815, and forged his way back to France. On March 20th he landed in Paris and resumed power—although it was ephemeral. He then set out for what was later to be known as his Hundred Days Campaign.

Wary of Napoleon's return, Austria, Britain, Prussia, and Russia formed alliances and prepared for war.

Napoleon, unmatched in his military skills, engineered a military plan to attack each country separately. His preemptive strike on Belgium in June 16th, 1815 defeated the Prussian arm—but failed to completely destroy it.

Two days later (June 18th, 1815) Napoleon and his army of 72,000 troops marched towards the British army of 68,000 men stationed at the South of Brussels adjacent to the village of Waterloo. This battle was titled as the Battle of Waterloo.

The British army was comprised of Dutch, German, and Belgium troops; it was led by Arthur Wellington (1769-1852).

The French army managed to formidably attack the British troops but the arrival of Prussian troops tipped the balance, forcing Napoleon to meet his Waterloo.

Wellington moved on to become Britain's Prime Minister.

Victorian Britain

The Great Exhibition — 1851

The Great Exhibition was a global exhibition which was carried out in Hyde Park London, from 1 may to 11 October, 1851. The Great Exhibition which was housed in the Crystal Palace was organized by Henry Cole and the husband of Queen Victoria, Prince Albert.

Charles Darwin, Samuel colt, Charlotte Bontë, Charles Dickens, Lewis Carroll, and George Eliot were amongst the numerous notable figures who attended the Crystal Palace Exhibition.

The Exhibition

There were some 100,000 objects, presented along more than 10 miles, by over 15,000 exhibitors. As host, Britain held half the display space inside, with exhibits from the home country and the Empire.

The Construction

The most magnificent exhibit of all was the building itself, which was designed by Joseph Paxton. Paxton used modules of glass and iron for his creative design, which could be fabricated offsite and afterwards dismantled again, as the construction was only temporary. On August

1850 the work began. By December more than 2000 men were working on the site. 80 men were able to fix over 8000 panes of sheet glass in a week and much more through the incredible machines invented by Paxton.

The Visitors

Queen Victoria opened the grand Exhibition on schedule on 1 May, 1851. There were over 6 million visitors by the time the Exhibition ended on October 11. Queen Victoria herself frequently visited the site. The price for admission initially was £3 for gentlemen, £2 for ladies. Saturday mornings were reserved for invalids. From 24th May, the masses were let in for only a shilling a head.And they arrived in thousands: country villagers sent by kind landowners, factory workers sent by their employers, strings of school children.

The Great Exhibition netted a profit of about £186,000, despite the loss initially predicted. The revenue was then used to buy the land in Kensington. And on this land, great museums were erected— the Victoria and Albert Museum were but a few.

The Crimean War — 1854

It was between 1853 and 1856 that the Crimean War took place. The three-year war was chiefly fought on the Crimean peninsula, hence its name. It was a conflict in which Russia was defeated to an alliance of France, Britain, Ottoman Turkish and Sardinia.

The immediate grounds of dispute involved the infringement of rights of Christian minorities in the Holy Land— a land controlled by the Ottoman Empire. The rights of the Catholics were highly encouraged by the French, while Russia encouraged that of the orthodox Christians.

Another major factor, this one being the long-term, was the deterioration of the Ottoman Empire and the reluctance of France and Britain to permit Russia to obtain power and area at the Ottoman Empire.

On the Russo-Turkish border, the Turks, backed by Britain, announced their stand against the Russians, who invaded the Danubian Principalities (modern Romania) in 1853. On September 23, the British fleet was dispatched to Constantinople (Istanbul).

The Turks waged war on Russia on October 4 and in that very same month launched an attack on the Russians in Danubian Principalities. To safeguard the Turkish transports, the French and British Fleets went into the Black Sea on the 3rd January, 1854, after the Russian Black Sea navy obliterated a Turkish troop at Sinope.

France and Britain waged war on Russia on March 28.

Fearing Austria would also join the war, Russia abandoned the Danubian Principalities. In August 1854, Austria occupied them. The allies, on September 1854, grounded troops in Russian Crimea, and commenced a yearlong siege of the Sevastopol – the Russian fortress.

The End of the War

The conflict in the Crimean war decreased a great deal after Sevastopol fell under the control of the allies. The Russians managed to sustain their power in Kars, but it wasn't long before the Ottoman Empire took the city back.

The bloody war lasted longer than expected which, especially for Britain, had occasioned disgruntlement at home. However, the ally threat stayed in Russian territories until the congress of Paris commenced on 1stFebruary, 1856. Finally, on March 30th, 1856, the Treaty of Paris was signed officially concluding the war.

The Last Public Hanging — 1868

Public execution ceased in 1868 as numerous people found it incredibly inhumane and it no longer acted as a deterrent factor for other criminals.

The last person who was publicly hanged in Britain was Michael Barret at Newgate. He was convicted of engaging in the lethal explosion that detonated outside Clerkenwell Prison in London on the 13th of December, 1867. It was an attempt to release Richard O'Sullivan Burke, a Fenian Brotherhood member. In the 19th century, the Clerkenwell bombing was the most dangerous terrorist act conducted by the Irish Republicans in Britain.

The bomb left a massive hole in the wall of the prison, obliterating and destroying a lot of houses near the prison in Corporation Lane. The explosion killed seven innocent people and injured several more. This was a bombing that the Irish carried out in England. 6 people were apprehended but Barret was the only offender that was sentenced to death at the Old Bailey on 6th April 1868.

Twenty seven year old Barret was hanged shortly after 8 a.m. on Tuesday, the 26th of May, 1868. The Times newspaper described the scenery of the public execution stating that there was a vast audience present including women and children of the lower class.

On 29th of May, three days later, the Capital Punishment (Amendment) Act was enacted ending public executions such as hangings, and commanding all executions to be finalized inside prison walls. It also required the attendance of the governor, sheriff or undersheriff, the prison doctor and other prison officers.

Education Act — 1870

The 1870 Education Act in Britain happens to be the earliest perhaps the first legislation dealing with the condition of education.

The motive behind the Act was the need for Britain to remain competitive in the world by being at the pole position of manufacture and improvement.

Schools were permitted to continue unchanged by the Education Act, but set up an administrative system of "school boards" to erect and administer schools in places where its much needed. The boards were made up of locally elected bodies and they would draw their funding from the local rates. The Board schools were managed by them.

These Boards were to provide elementary education for children aged 5-13 (inclusive). Unlike the charitable schools, religious teaching in the board schools was 'non-denominational'.

The school remained fee-charging, so parents still had to pay for their children to attend school; nevertheless, parents who were poor were exempted as the school board paid for their children's fee.

The Act was not adapted until later years through firm reforms. There were people who opposed the concept of universal education, believing that handing children to a central authority could lead to indoctrinations, while others feared that mass education would equip people to scam those who were uneducated.

Population of Britain 40 million — 1901

Life expectancy of children, during the Industrial Revolution dramatically soared. The number of children born in London who have died before the age of five reduced from 74.5 per thousand in 1730- 1749 to 31.8 per thousand in 1810-1829.

In the West, population growth increased more rapidly after the advent of vaccination and other advances in sanitation and medicine. These improvements helped the population of Britain increase from 10 million to 40 million by 1901.

Modern Britain

World War I — 1914-1918

Britain's entry in the First World War commenced when the Liberal Party's British Prime Minister, Henry Asquith, declared war on the German Empire.

Britain was never bound by any obligations to support France or Russia in a war with Germany, and she was expected to stay neutral. But it was evident to the powers-that-be that the domination of a hostile European power would threaten the welfare of the English Channels. And in seek of a bargain that could curtail the calamities of war, the British Foreign Secretary Sir Edward Grey, repeatedly called upon Germany to host a conference and seek out a peaceful solution with the Great powers. Germany, however, refused and ended giving Britain a deadline to pick a stand –11 p.m., August 4th, 1914.

Britain became part of the Allied or Entente powers (France, Great Britain, Russia, Serbia, Belgium, Japan, and Montenegro) mainly as a sea power, and the combat against the Central Powers (the Austro-Hungarian Empire, the German Empire, the Kingdom of Bulgaria and the Ottoman Empire) commenced.

The war went on viciously for the following four years, claiming thirty-three million lives and resources that strained the western world for generations to come. The war with Germany was officially concluded after the signing of the Treaty of Versailles.

The death toll of British soldiers during this war reached 850,000. The war, irrefutably did have a severe side effect on Britain, amongst which were the first aerial bombardments of the cities in Britain. But it was also a contributing factor in the future development and unity of the nation as a whole.

During the war nationalism surged deep within society. And because of the penetrating propaganda issued by the newspapers, the supporters of the war increased tremendously. Volunteering soldiers, who were commonly known as Kitchener's Army, reached about 400,000 from 1914-1915. This was also the period in which Britain declared the supremacy of the Royal Navy and when the Royal Flying Corps (RFC) and the Royal Naval Air Service (RNAS) were amalgamated to form the new Royal Air Force (RAF).

Ireland's Declaration of Independence — 1920

Home rule had been the primary objective of Irish nationalists ever since the 1880s. But their objective took years before it came into being, and it was only after a long and bloody struggle that Ireland became a republic in 1920.

The Irish nationalists' progress was laggard mainly because of the many thwarting events Britain was involved in, one of which being the World War I. But then a turning point came when the British parliament, impelled by the pressure of dealing with the crises brought on by the German Spring Offensive in 1918, attempted to pass on a conscription linked with Home Rule in Ireland. It was initially a highly contested imposition, but the War Cabinet still pursued it.

This conscription was never enforced, but it did manage to fuel the Irish people's already flaring desire for independence.

Outraged, members of the Irish Parties at Westminster walked out of parliament in protest and went back to Ireland to propagate opposition. A mass demonstration was then held on the 23rd of April, 1918— nearly everyone participated. Thereafter, separation from British rule became a matter that the majority of the Irish people conclusively wanted.

Then in the 1918 general election, Irish electorates declared their stand by giving 70 percent of the Irish Seats to the Nationalists party, Sin Féin— it was a landslide victory.

Sin Féin then publicly pledged not to ever convene in the UK parliament at Westminster. And on January 21st, 1919, the first parliament, called the First Dáil, was established in Ireland at the Mansion House. The ministers were called the Aireacht, and it consisted of Sinn Féin members only.

The Dáil then soon affirmed the Declaration of Independence and sent out a message to the 'Free Nations of the World' stating that Ireland and England were in a state of war. On that very day two police officers were gunned down at county Tipperary, which according to historians signaled the dawn of the Irish War of Independence.

The battle between the Irish Republican Army and the British Army Patrols was bloody and it resulted in a devastating amount of casualties that devastated the lives of many civilians.

Then on July 11, 1921, there was a cease fire on both ends, which was soon followed by the signing of the Anglo-Irish Treaty on December 6th 1921.

Then, after the transitional period of ten months, on December 6th 1922, the Irish Free State came into formation.

World War II — 1939-1945

In 1938, Britain endeavored to pacify Germany in hope to avoid seeing another world war. To accomplish just that, the Munich Pact was signed, "Permitting" Germany to occupy the disputed Czechoslovakia's land— Sudetenland. However, the peace that England was attempting to accomplish was rendered futile when Hitler, just a few months later, occupied the rest of Czechoslovakia.

Although Britain announced its integrity to Poland if Germany invaded it, Germany invaded anyway. (There was a covert pact signed between Stalin and Hitler which divided Poland between the two dictatorships).

Britain publicly waged war on Germany in 1939, on 3rd September. This signaled the dawn of WWII in Europe. The inhabitants of Britain suffered greatly during the war in 1940, from July to October —there was an intense Bombing by Germany. However, Britain was safeguarded by the Royal Air Force from the Luftwaffe.

Through the Lend-Lease Act, the U.S. began providing war materials, foodstuffs, and clothing in March 1941 to Britain.

In December, following the Pearl Harbor, America directly began to support the British. Franklin Roosevelt and Winston Churchill, in January 1942, decided to institute a Combined Chiefs of Staff (CCS) to make Germany on top of their list.

Three years later, the Allies won the war in Europe. On May 7, 1945, Germany surrendered unconditionally. The casualties of soldiers of Great Britain accounted for 300,000 and the casualties of civilians accounted for over 60,000.

Britain's partaking in the Gulf War — 1990

The Gulf War, which is also known as the Persian Gulf War (1990-1991), came in to formation when Iraq's leader, Saddam Hussein, decided to violate international law and invade Kuwait on August 2, 1990.

In the light of the situation the United Nations Security Council immediately called for the withdrawal of Iraq from Kuwait on August 3rd, 1990. When Iraq wouldn't comply, the Council issued a worldwide ban in trade with Iraq.

In response to this sanction, Iraq's leader, Saddam Hussein, officially declared the annexation of Kuwait on August 8th. At this juncture, the United States along with its Western European NATO allies, marched to Saudi Arabia to curtail any attacks directed to Saudi or other neighboring countries in the Middle East.

During this war the United Kingdom went forth with committing the largest contingent from any other European participants in the combat's operations.

The British military operations in the Persian Gulf War went by its code name, Operation Granby. This operation was named after Jhon Manners, Marquees of Granby, and commander of the British force at the Battle of Minden in 1756.

The British contribution in the Persian Gulf War included the British Army regiments, the Royal Navy and Royal fleet Auxiliary ships, and the Royal Air Force Squadrons. Britain committed about 2,500 armored vehicles and deployed to about 43,000 troops.

The Channel Tunnel — 1994

"The French and the British peoples, for all their individual diversity and ages-long rivalry, complement each other well – better perhaps than we realize"

– Queen Elizabeth II

The channel tunnel or Eurotunnel is amongst the most laudable engineering accomplishments in the history of Europe.

The construction of this tunnel took about six years to complete (1988-1994) and it cost over £4 billion. The project was first envisioned and proposed by a French engineer, Albert Mathieu, in 1802. And legions of similar proposals were also presented on the following years, but none, including Albert's were accepted, primarily for safety reasons. But after World War II and the presentation of a geological survey in 1964-1965 that came right after, the project ended up gaining the support of the French and British government.

Then in 1974, construction on both ends of the channel began.

The tunnel was inaugurated on May 6th, 1994 by Queen Elizabeth II and the French President M. Mitterrand. This project wasn't only an exceeding accomplishment in the world of engineering, but also an impetus that the whole of Europe needed to strengthen the strained diplomatic relation.

"This is the first time that the heads of state of France and Britain have been able to meet each other without either of them having to travel by sea or by air," the Queen said on the day of the inauguration.

During this inauguration President M. Mitterrand also voiced his belief in the tunnel having the potential of uniting Europe.

The Eurotunnel or Tunnel Channel is a 50.5 Kilometer rail tunnel that links Folkston, Kent, in the United Kingdom with Conquelles, Pas-de-Calais, in Northern France. The tunnel lies beneath the English Channel at the Strait of Dover.

Currently, up to 400 trains pass through the tunnel each day, carrying up to 50,000 passengers, 180 coaches, 54,000 tons of freight and 6,000 cars.

The lining of the tunnel is designed to last for about 120 years.

Printed in Great Britain
by Amazon